Because I Love You

Because I Love You

Alice Joyce Davidson

Fleming H. Revell Company
Old Tappan, New Jersey

Scripture quotations are from the King James Version of the Bible.

Library of Congress Cataloging in Publication Data

Davidson, Alice Joyce.
  Because I love you.

    1. Religious poetry, American.   I. Title.
PS3554.A922B4   811'.54   81-10585
  ISBN 0-8007-1281-1   AACR2

Dedicated to the memory of Helen Steiner Rice, my dear friend and co-worker, who encouraged me with her friendship and inspired me by her beautiful examples of loving, living, and giving.

Contents

Publisher's Note

As this book entered the final stages of production, Helen Steiner Rice embarked on her journey "home." Throughout her long and difficult illness, the indomitable spirit of this remarkable and talented woman continued to shine, bringing cheer and comfort to all whose lives she touched. Mrs. Rice was eager to see this book published. It was she who inspired and encouraged the writer. Mrs. Rice's introduction follows.

The Publisher

10

Introduction

It is both a privilege and a pleasure to introduce to you Alice Joyce Davidson, a dear friend and close business associate at Gibson Greeting Cards. I have known her for almost two decades and during that period have enjoyed our chatting and philosophizing about human nature, brotherhood, and—more importantly—the goodness of God.

Alice is extremely talented as an artist, as you will see in the ensuing pages. She is equally gifted as a writer of poems. It is in this latter regard that I would ask you to share some of my thoughts about poems and poets.

What is a poem?

How many times I have asked myself that question.

What *is* a poem?

Is it more than a grouping of words, rhyming or not, pithy or poignant, simple or sophisticated?

Is it the "communication ... of a complete experience," to borrow from Webster's definition?

I would agree with that, at least in part. But I would go a bit beyond, for it is my belief that a poem is a giving, living entity.

It lifts the shadows and illuminates the substance.

It offers hope and negates despair.

It recalls a precious memory yet projects another.

Above all, it is a personal message—sometimes light-hearted, sometimes deeply penetrating.

It can be inspiring or introspective, almost like a silent friend, a knowing comforter.

And who is a poet?

I suppose a qualified or qualifying description would be any-
one who puts pen to paper and achieves the above. But is
achievement so easily marked?

No. Clearly there is a Source beyond the individual.

He offers His gift. He is a presence.

I know.

I have felt Him permeate my thoughts. I have listened to
Him.

He has been my sole—my *soul's*—inspiration.

To me, writing poetry has not been a pastime, a diversion. It
has been a ministry. I have been so blessed in my lifetime, and
I am deeply grateful to Him.

The challenge remains open to all who would hear Him and
accept it.

One who has heeded and accepted this charge is Alice Joyce
Davidson.

This woman's talent and artistry and dedication need no further
embellishment from me. And so, with fondest wishes and highest
hopes for the spreading of His word through hers, I now introduce
this poet and her poems.

Prologue

> I'll entrust the Lord above
> To especially bless you with His love
> And in His holy way convey
> What I so much would like to say
> As "memory paints in colors so true"
> The wonderful friendship I've shared with you!

These words have a special meaning to me for two reasons—they remind me of the beautiful friendship I was lucky to have, and they came from the pen of my dear friend. They were written by the late Helen Steiner Rice, the Poet Laureate of Inspirational verse. This book is dedicated to Mrs. Rice as a tribute to her friendship and in appreciation of her influence and inspiration.

Mrs. Rice and I had neighboring offices at the same greeting card company. She was the star of the inspirational lines, while I have "twinkled" off and on in the humorous field. I like to make people laugh—I love to make people happy. But nothing gives me more satisfaction than writing from the soul. When this book began to develop, Mrs. Rice encouraged me with her interest and generous words of praise, such as this: ". . . these three verses are terrific. You are getting better and better, so all your efforts have paid off in 'glory to God!' "

When I told Mrs. Rice that I was dedicating this book to her and asked if she had a few words for my prologue, she gave this to me:

> Helen Steiner Rice says of Alice Joyce Davidson. . . .
> "She speaks from her heart in a special way, and in her special style she opens 'new doors' to God!"

It is my hope that as you read my book you will feel happy, and you will be reminded of the many ways you know love and show love. It is my prayer that feelings of peace, goodness, and loving-kindness will spread near and far so we may all know a oneness with each other—a oneness with God!

Sing unto him a new song . . .
the earth is full of the good-
ness of the Lord.

Psalms 33:3,5

Sing God's Praises

When I look at God's flowers
Or feel His cool breeze,
Or taste the sweet gifts
From His fruit-bearing trees . . .
      My heart sings!

When I study the stars
That light up the sky,
Or watch a young fledgling
Just learning to fly . . .
      My heart sings!

When I marvel at nature,
Each miracle of
God's awesome creation
He fashioned with love . . .
      My heart sings!

And, when my heart's singing,
I offer a prayer
Of thanks for His bountiful gifts
Which I share,
And as I am praying,
I feel His great care . . .
      And my heart sings!

In Harmony With Nature

There are wonders all around us
To see, to touch, to hear—
God's handiwork surrounds us
And reminds us He is near . . .
So every time you smell a flower,
Or see a starlit sky,
Or hear a cricket chirping,
Or feel a breeze blow by,
Or witness all the splendor
A changing season brings,
You've touched the hand of God above—
The Creator of all things!

**And the Lord God formed man of the dust
of the ground. . . .**

Genesis 2:7

Look to Each New Day

A blaze of light
   streaks through the darkened sky
     melting grayness into pink.
A new day begins . . .
   a new day to walk into life.
Thank You, God, for Your gift of a new day
   a new opportunity
     to do, to feel . . .
       to be.

**This is the day which the Lord hath made;
we will rejoice and be glad in it.**

Psalms 118:24

Give Hope to Others

We all have our rainy days
when the clouds are so thick
it's hard to find the way
by ourselves

Unless we have an umbrella
  an umbrella of faith and hope.

When I see someone standing
lost in a storm,
help me, God, to remember
to offer my umbrella
  my umbrella of faith and hope.

**He giveth power to the faint;
and to them that have no
might he increaseth strength.**

Isaiah 40:29

Say a Prayer

Prayers are thoughts
turned Godward.

Silent thoughts,
spoken thoughts,
thoughts expressed in song,
shout-happy-Hallelujah thoughts
and clap your hands along!

Prayers are thoughts
turned Godward.

Thoughts of thanks,
and hope and faith,
and love beyond compare—
and when a thought turns Godward
it becomes a heartfelt prayer!

Pray without ceasing.

1 Thessalonians 5:17

In Nature's Arms

Leaves were budding,
Birds were singing,
Fawns were feeding,
Spring was springing . . .
When I walked the other day
Through a winding wooded way . . .
Chipmunks chattered,
Squirrels were scolding,
Ferns unfurled,
Flowers unfolding . . .
And, while wrapped in Nature's arms,
Beguiled by her many charms,
I found such peace and beauty there,
I thanked God with a quiet prayer!

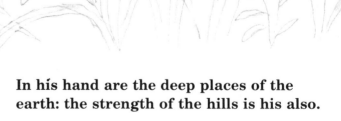

**In his hand are the deep places of the
earth: the strength of the hills is his also.**

Psalms 95:4

Spread God's Word

Sometimes
I want to shout
with glee—
"Hey everybody,
look at me—
I found God!"

I found Him
in the warmth of friendship
in the joy of giving
I found Him
in loving
in laughing—
in living!

I found God
And you can find Him, too—
Just open up your heart
and God will come
        to YOU!

**And he said unto them, Go ye
into all the world, and preach
the gospel to every creature.**

Mark 16:15

But his delight is in the law of the
Lord; and in his law doth he meditate
day and night.

Psalms 1:2

Meditation

I sat down by a crystal spring,
My back against a willow tree,
The sound of waters murmuring
Brought peace and restfulness to me
And letting go of everything
I closed my eyes . . . so I could "see"
And in that meditative hour,
I knew God's love and felt His power.

Blessed is the nation whose God is the Lord;
and the people whom he hath chosen for
his own inheritance.

Psalms 33:12

Cherish Freedom

Because I am an American,
  I know the sounds of freedom.
    From songs and words of adoration and praise
    to harsh criticism spewn out in anger,
    I know every sound
      and I am free to listen, to tune out,
        to speak up, or be silent.

Because I am an American,
  I know the sights of freedom.
    From the glitter of a holiday parade
    to a handmade protester's sign,
    I know every sight
      and I am free to observe, to ignore,
        to show myself, or be hidden.

Because I am an American,
  I know the feeling of freedom—
    the joy, the excitement,
      the fever, the agony,
        the anger, the quiver,
          the swell, the thrill,
          the pride.

Because I am an American,
  I have no bounds.
    I can soar as high
    as I have the strength and the will
    to soar.
    I can create or do nothing.
    I can be anything I want to be.
    I can be me.
    I can be.
      Because I am an American!

Listen to a Songbird

Little bird perched in the tree
Where did you get your melody?
Who taught your little breast to swell
With tones unrivaled by a bell?
Who put the gladness in each note
That comes so sweetly from your throat?

With a cock of the head that was almost a nod
The little bird answered by singing . . . to God!

**The flowers appear on the earth; the time
of the singing of birds is come . . . .**

Song of Solomon 2:12

To God, With Love

Dear God,
    This is the first time ever that
I've written You a letter . . . but I just had
to thank You, now that everything is better.

    I came to You a while back so troubled
and distressed, I didn't know what course to
take, what action would be best . . . I told You
all my troubles, and I felt Your presence near . . .
and as I talked the clouds broke up and seemed
to disappear.

    So, thank You, God, for listening, for
keeping me from harm, for wiping tears and holding
me within Your loving arms.

**Come unto me, all ye that labour and are heavy
laden, and I will give you rest.**

Matthew 11:28

The Summit

A mountain climber
sets his sights on the top.

With courage, with faith
he overcomes fear and fatigue
until he reaches the summit
and in reaching the summit
has his reward.

So it is in life.

Those who reach the summit—
those who have their reward with the Lord—
overcame a mountain!

For our light affliction, which is but for
a moment, worketh for us a far more
exceeding and eternal weight of glory.

2 Corinthians 4:17

Faith Is the Key

What is the key to true success?
The key to joy and happiness?
Faith is!
Faith in yourself to make a start
And follow dreams within your heart,
And faith in God to be beside you
To light your way and always guide you . . .
Faith will open doors for you
Faith will make your dreams come true
So, never fear to try a scheme,
To make a plan, to dream a dream,
For dreams become reality
If you remember that the key
To everything you want to be
Is FAITH!

**Though thy beginning was small, yet
thy latter end should
greatly increase.**

Job 8:7

Welcome, Baby

Welcome, baby, welcome,
It's so nice to have you here—
Your innocence and sweetness
Bring a bit of heaven near . . .
Welcome, baby, welcome,
May life be good to you,
May your days be bright and sunny,
May your skies above be blue,
May you grow in love and learn to love
Everyone around you,
And always, may God bless you
And may happiness surround you!

**And God blessed them, and God said
unto them, Be fruitful, and multiply. . . .**

Genesis 1:28

Happiness Comes

God laughs
in sunbeams

golden sunbeams
of love
of hope
of faith

and when
His golden sunbeams
dance upon
your heart

happiness comes.

**Rejoice in the Lord alway:
and again I say, Rejoice.**

Philippians 4:4

Peace Within

Lord, I know the road to peace
      is filled with rocks and holes.
How can nations travel the road
      when neighbors find it difficult
         and brothers often stumble?

Help me take the first step, Lord,
      help me find the way
         to peace within myself.

. . . but to the counsellors of peace is joy.

Proverbs 12:20

32

Moving Forward

Easy morals
   easy values
      temptations all around us . . .
Should *we* change
   or should we change
      the looseness that surrounds us?

The world is changing
   making progress
      moving forward day by day . . .
But our souls
   will progress only
      if we follow in God's way!

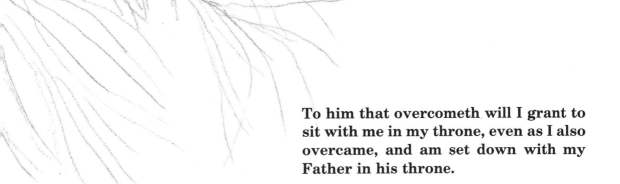

To him that overcometh will I grant to sit with me in my throne, even as I also overcame, and am set down with my Father in his throne.

Revelation 3:21

Be kindly affectioned one to another with
brotherly love; in honour preferring one another.

Romans 12:10

Roots of Love

All who share God's kingdom,
All humanity,
All of us together
Are part of one great tree . . .

We branch out, and we blossom,
We bear our fruit and grow,
And as we're branching, growing, reaching,
Somehow we still know . . .

That all of us together,
All humanity,
Share one root—one root of love
For all eternity!

Faith

There's hope for each of us with faith,
There's hope for all who trod
Within His light, within His love,
Within the path of God,
For those of us who realize
With both our minds and hearts,
That whatever may befall us,
Whatever life imparts,
We only have to stretch our hand
To Him who dwells up high
And He will give us guidance,
He will show us by and by
That faith and trust will always
Take us through the darkest night,
And prayer that's said in earnest
Will shed the brightest light.

. . . I am the light of the world; he
that followeth me shall not
walk in darkness, but shall have
the light of life.

John 8:12

Be Thankful

Thank You, Lord,
for Your beautiful works
that surround me . . .

Thank You, Lord
for the power of Your love
that fills me . . .

Thank You, Lord,
for shedding Your light
on my path!

**It is a good thing to give thanks
unto the Lord. . . .**

Psalms 92:1

Be Even Tempered

Before you lose your temper,
Take a breath and count to ten,
And silently ask God to help you
Gain control again . . .
And have a pardon handy
For the errors others make,
Offer love and understanding,
And banish hate and ache . . .
Be even tempered always,
Be loving and forgiving,
And you will be rewarded
With peace and joyful living!

**He that is slow to wrath is of
great understanding: but he
that is hasty of spirit exalteth folly.**

Proverbs 14:29

A Whiff of Lilacs

I just had a whiff
a great, big wonderful whiff
of lilacs blooming everywhere . . .
and just like bubbles
my troubles
vanished
in thin
air.

Thank You, God,
for the joy of Your fragrant flowers!

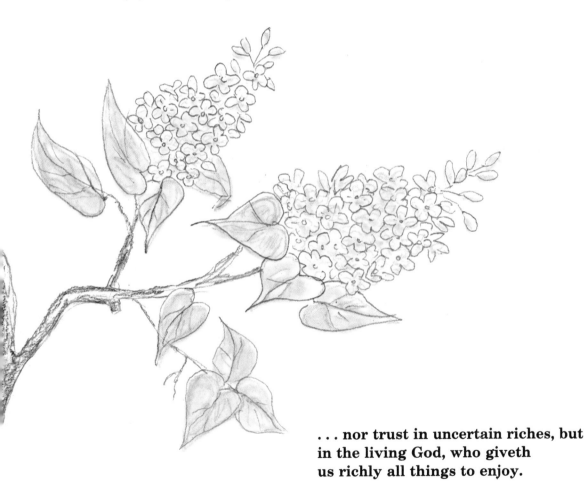

. . . nor trust in uncertain riches, but
in the living God, who giveth
us richly all things to enjoy.

1 Timothy 6:17

Follow Him

There are many roads to take in life,
Roads of peace and roads of strife
Throughout our long sojourn,
And, when we come to roads that cross,
We sometimes feel we're at a loss
Not certain where to turn,
But if we ask our Lord to guide us
To light our path and walk beside us
We've no need for concern,
For God who made both land and sea,
Mapped the way for you and me
To live with Him eternally
After Life's sojourn!

**I am the good shepherd, and know
my sheep, and am known of mine.**

John 10:14

Be Virtuous

Step by step
Deed by deed
Kindness by kindness

Lord, help me climb
The stairway to Heaven

Lord, help me walk
closer to You!

**And beside this, giving all
diligence, add to your faith
virtue; and to virtue knowledge.**

2 Peter 1:5

Two Together

A happy groom, a happy bride
Smiling, walking side by side
    Together
        down a brand new road in life
Hand in hand they'll walk together
Through sunny and through stormy weather
And, though they'll have some hills to climb,
God will be close all the time
To answer every prayer they pray
And help them as they go their way
    Together
        down a brand new road in life!

And the Lord God said, It is not good that the man should be alone; I will make him an help meet for him.

Genesis 2:18

Understand His Purpose

There's a purpose for each petal
That graces every flower,
There's a purpose to each second
In each minute in each hour,
There's a purpose to each sunrise
That lights the sky each day—
And a purpose to each trial
We find along life's way,
And although a purpose might not be
Revealed at once to man,
Nothing in God's kingdom
Is without a perfect plan!

The wisdom of the prudent is to understand his way. . . .

Proverbs 14:8

My son, if sinners entice thee, consent thou not.

Proverbs 1:10

Crossroads

I want to ask You, Dear God,
about freedom,
about freedom
in making a choice . . .
How will I know
to be silent,
or to raise
an inquiring voice? . . .

How will I know
when I'm right or I'm wrong,
when to back down
and when to be strong?

I want to talk to You, God
about freedom,
about freedom
to make a mistake.
How will I know
what direction to go
when there's so many
pathways to take?

Could I travel a road
that's out of Your sight?
Is there anywhere, God,
that's not lit by Your light?

Is the answer, Dear God,
to my freedom—
this awesome
responsible thing—
That You want me to grow
and You want me to know
every facet that living
can bring?

The Magic of a Smile

A smile is
a magic thing

you can keep it
and pass it on to others
at the same time

a smile can
erase sadness
alleviate loneliness
and even cure a headache

a smile is
a ray of sun
a show of love
a gift that comes right back to you
a blessing from above!

Thou hast put gladness in my heart. . . .

Psalms 4:7

Enjoy Work

A mother rocks a cradle
With a smile on her face . . .
An astronaut hums softly
As he charts his way in space . . .
A surgeon heaves a thankful sigh
As another life is saved . . .
A construction worker chuckles
As he drives on roads he paved . . .
God gives a special task to do
To each and everyone
And blesses us with special joy
Each time a job's well done!

**The sleep of a labouring man is
sweet, whether he eat little or much. . . .**

Ecclesiastes 5:12

Pathways

If everyone was a poet
fields would be sown with sonnets,
babies clothed with lullabies,
and pathways would be paved with parables!
How wise of You, God,
to give each of us
different talents
different tools
to turn Your wonderful words,
Your wondrous works
into living poetry!

Whatsoever thy hand findeth to do, do it
with thy might. . . .

Ecclesiastes 9:10

Discover Yourself

There are many things
in God's Universe
waiting to be discovered.

There are stars to be named
cures to be found
new vistas to be explored.

But the most wonderful discovery of all
is the discovery
of oneself.

So God created man in his own image. . . .

Genesis 1:27

For Ever and Ever

A lifetime on earth
in the endlessness of eternity
is like a grain of sand
on a never-ending beach.

No matter how small it may seem,
the grain of sand has a purpose.
It can reflect the warmth
of the sun,
hold back the tide,
or become part of a beautiful sand castle.

No matter how brief it may seem,
a life on earth has purpose.
It can reflect the warmth
of God's love,
hold back the forces of evil,
and become a part of His glorious kingdom
forever.

With long life will I satisfy him. . . .

Psalms 91:16

Brighter Views

Flowers bloom . . . and songbirds sing
In happy ecstasy—
The world is filled with gladness,
That's how God meant it to be,
And He gave us capabilities
To add a special glow
And bring a bit of happiness
To those we love and know . . .
So every time you help someone
To see a brighter view,
Or bring a happy smile so that
The sun comes shining through,
You please God for you've done what He
Intended you to do!

A merry heart maketh a cheerful
countenance. . . .

Proverbs 15:13

By My Side

Dear God,
with
You
at
my
side
I'm not afraid to dream.

With
You
at
my
side
I'm not afraid to try.

With
You
at
my
side
I'm not afraid to succeed!

**Delight thyself also in the Lord;
and he shall give thee the
desires of thine heart.**

Psalms 37:4

From Darkness to Light

"The Lord is thy keeper"
And in Him you'll find
Strength to renew
The body and mind . . .
For He is our refuge
From all kinds of harms,
He protects us and holds us
Within loving arms,
He turns tears to smiles,
Darkness to light,
And if things go wrong,
He will make them all right.
And whenever you need Him,
He always is there—
"The Lord is thy keeper"
And you're in His care.

Heal me, O Lord, and I shall
be healed. . . .

Jeremiah 17:14

In God's Light

To believe in God
is to turn on a light.

The more you believe,
the brighter the light becomes
illuminating your life
bringing sunshine to your soul.

**I am come a light into the world,
that whosoever believeth on
me should not abide in darkness.**

John 12:46

Bring Tomorrow's Dawning

If I have failed to do a thoughtful deed,
Or turned my back on anyone in need,
If I've ignored the clouds in someone's skies,
Or missed the chance to wipe another's eyes,
If I have spoken words of bitterness,
If I have failed or faltered, more or less,
If I've forgotten the golden rule someway—
Lord, bring tomorrow's dawning, so I may
Make up for all I've left undone today!

**Therefore all things whatsoever ye would
that men should do to you, do ye even so
to them: for this is the law and the prophets.**

Matthew 7:12

Individuality

All of us are blessed with
Individuality,
We're different from each other—
That's how God meant us to be,
So when opinions differ,
And you don't see eye to eye,
Or angry words are spoken
And tempers start to fly,
Calm yourself and try to see
The other person's view—
Mediate your differences
As God wants you to do,
For by living well with others
Through every kind of strife,
Our horizons broaden
And we get much more from life!

Be ye angry, and sin not: let not the
sun go down upon your wrath.

Ephesians 4:26

Brighten the World for Others

Thank You, Lord,
for showing me
that happiness is all a matter
of degree.

To find happiness
    is good.

To create happiness
    is better.

But to bring happiness to others,
    that's the best, Lord,
        the very best!

**Let your light so shine before
men, that they may see your
good works, and glorify
your Father, which is in heaven.**

Matthew 5:16

This is the Lord's doing; it is
marvellous in our eyes.

Psalms 118:23

Wonder at His Workings

God's beauty pervades the earth

It glistens in the waves
   of the sea

gleams in the stars
   in the sky

beguiles in the smile
   of a babe

How He must love us
   to give us such
      glorious gifts!

Let Go to God

Dear God,
It isn't easy to be captain of my own ship
on the sea of life
because, God, sometimes the waters are filled
with turbulence and strife.
But I know I can calm a billowing wave
and bring peace to the stormiest sea
when I let Your spirit that dwells within
take over my ship for me!

**Know ye not that ye are the temple
of God, and that the Spirit of God
dwelleth in you?**

1 Corinthians 3:16

Be Patient

I know
I can't pick a bouquet
of daisies in the winter—
I wait till the time
is right.

Dear God,
why then can't I learn
patience with things that matter
and wait till the time
is right?

**Now the God of patience and
consolation grant you to be
likeminded. . . .**

Romans 15:5

Give Freely

God is a giver
of all things
wonderful and wise.

In love
He gives of Himself.

Then He gives us compassion
so that we might likewise
give of ourselves
in love.

Give, and it shall be given unto you. . . .

Luke 6:38

Be Kind

Just a little bit of kindness
Can go a long, long way,
Just a little bit of tenderness
Can brighten up a day.

Just a bit of praise where it's deserved
Can bring a happy glow,
Just a hand held out can give some hope
To someone feeling low.

A forgiving word, a handshake,
A pat upon the head,
Can take away a heavy heart
And bring a smile instead.

Just a little bit of kindness
Can go a long, long way
In reflecting the benevolence
God shows us every day!

And be ye kind one to another. . . .

Ephesians 4:32

A Wealth of Wisdom

On a stoop of a porch
they sit and wait.
An old woman and man
each without a mate.

They sit together,
yet they are alone.

They talk for hours, on and on
of friends and loved ones who have gone,
of childhood days, their fathers and mothers.
Neither listens to the other—
by now their stories are old and tired, too.

Yet, what a wealth of wisdom, Lord,
each of them has to share
with anyone who takes the time
to spend a minute there.
But most of the time they just sit and wait
hoping for someone to open their gate.

They shall still bring forth fruit in old age. . . .

Psalms 92:14

Friendship

What is a friend?
    Someone to sigh with,
    Someone to cry with,
    To be with through smiles and woes,
    Someone to talk with,
    Someone to walk with
    Wherever a path in life goes.
    A friend is a treasure,
    An all around pleasure
    To share with, to care with and love.
    Wrapped with affection,
    And made to perfection,
    A friend is a gift from above!

A friend loveth at all times. . . .

Proverbs 17:17

No Greater Gift

Master of all living things—
Your ways are ways of love!
You gave us gifts of warmth and light,
You hung the sun above.

You gave us fertile fields to plow,
You gave us fruiting trees,
You gave us mountains to be climbed,
You gave us mighty seas.

You gave us challenges to meet
To fill our waking hours,
You even shared a glimpse with us
Of Your creative powers.

But the greatest gift You gave to us,
The gift we most extol,
Is the gift of life—eternal life—
An everlasting soul!

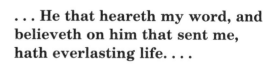

**. . . He that heareth my word, and
believeth on him that sent me,
hath everlasting life. . . .**

John 5:24

Contentment

You could search
the world over
and not find
contentment.

Contentment comes
when you stop searching
around yourself
and you start searching
within yourself
and you find your purpose
your soul
and God!

**But godliness with contentment
is great gain.**

1 Timothy 6:6

Praise Others

As we travel through life,
We all have our share
Of problems to solve,
And crosses to bear.
But when someone comes by
With some praise and a smile,
Our burdens seem lighter,
Our purpose worthwhile—
Oh, what a blessing
It is on life's road
When someone comes by
To lighten our load!

**Heaviness in the heart of man
maketh it stoop: but a good
word maketh it glad.**

Proverbs 12:25

Be Loving

To bring a bit of heaven
Down to earth from high above,
God blessed the world abundantly
With many kinds of love—
The love within a family,
The love of man and wife,
The love for creatures large and small,
And all that's good in life.
And every bit of love we show,
Each act of love we do,
Brings us closer yet to heaven
And to God who loves us, too!

... let us love one another: for love
is of God; and every one that loveth
is born of God, and knoweth God ...
for God is love.

1 John 4:7,8

Sunset Symphony

It comes . . .
every evening
without fanfare or drums
it comes . . .

it comes softly as a lullaby
beginning with a golden glow
encircling a cloud . . .

and then the glow begins to grow . . .
pinks and violets fill the sky
a ball of orange delights the eye
the cymbals crash, the trumpets blare
a symphony has filled the air,
a silent symphony!
Applause! Applause!
a spectacular show!

then the ball of orange, ablaze, aglow,
sinks slowly out of sight . . .

God has tucked away a day
and ushered in the night!

And God made two great lights; the greater
light to rule the day, and the lesser
light to rule the night. . . .

Genesis 1:16

Comfort the Bereaved

When earthbound
days are done
and loved ones
go beyond,
sometimes our Lord's promise
for eternal life
is hidden
in grief
and loneliness
and strife,
but a sympathetic nod,
a note that says, "I care,"
a gesture
or a hand to hold
will lift clouds
of despair.

**Rejoice with them that do rejoice, and
weep with them that weep.**

Romans 12:15

Work Toward Peace

Dear Father, I beseech Thee,
I implore Thee as I pray
To counsel me, to guide me
And help me find the way
To do my part in making
The world a better place,
Not only for my loved ones,
But for every creed and race,
And help me find the way to lift
The clouds of hate and fear
So, in the sunshine of Your love,
The path to peace is clear.

**Blessed are the peacemakers:
for they shall be called the
children of God.**

Matthew 5:9

Plant a Seed

Within a seed
    there's a beautiful flower,
And within a prayer
    there's a wonderful power . . .
And just as we must plant a seed
    to gather a bouquet,
To gather spiritual strength and grow,
    we must take time to pray.

In the morning sow thy seed. . . .

Ecclesiastes 11:6

Balancing

Sometimes
I feel
as if I'm walking a tightrope
and for a balance pole
I need control

control over my temper
control over my impulses
control over my emotions.

Help me keep my balance, Lord,
give me the patience, the power, the perspective
to gain more control
so that I can get from here to there
without falling.

**He that hath no rule over his own spirit is
like a city that is broken down, and
without walls.**

Proverbs 25:28

Follow God's Word

For inner satisfaction,
Contentment, peace of mind,
Read the Holy Bible
And in it you will find
A treasury of wisdom,
Advice of every kind . . .
There are answers to the problems
You encounter every day,
There are words of love and words of praise
To meditate and pray—
And every word you read will bring you
Closer to God's way!

. . . Seek ye out of the book of the Lord,
and read. . . .

Isaiah 34:16

Love the Unlovable

Sometimes
loneliness manifests itself
as coldness
heartache as bitterness
frustration as meanness.

Why is it we seem to act the most unlovable
when we need to be loved the most?

Help me, Lord, to see
past coldness
past bitterness
past meanness
and into the hearts of those
who need to be loved the most!

. . . If we love one another,
God dwelleth in us. . . .

1 John 4:12

Doing Deeds, Filling Needs

Life would surely be sublime
If everyone would take the time
To do a thoughtful deed,
Time to lend a listening ear,
To offer comfort, or send cheer
To someone who's in need . . .
And every burden you make lighter,
Every minute you make brighter,
Will make you happy, too,
Because good deeds are acts of love,
Beautiful reflections of
Our Father who dwells high above
And fondly blesses you!

**Withhold not good from them
to whom it is due, when it is in
the power of thine hand to do it.**

Proverbs 3:27

Insight

A molecule
a mountain
a dewdrop
an ocean

> All things great and small
> are of God
> All beings . . . we are all
> of God

And the wiser we grow
And the more that we know

> of all of His things
> of all of His beings
> the more we know of God.

**Wisdom is the principal thing;
therefore get wisdom: and with
all thy getting get understanding.**

Proverbs 4:7

Love Liberty

Freedom is the breath of life—
Oh, help us, God, to see
The days when oppression is no more—
When all know liberty,
When bondage of the soul, the mind,
Of nations, too, will cease,
When truth and love will flourish—
When Your peoples all know peace.

**But whoso looketh into the perfect law
of liberty, and continueth therein . . .
this man shall be blessed in his deed.**

James 1:25

Desire Good

I want to do what's good in life
And serve You faithfully,
So when I seek, please help me, Lord,
To clearly know and see,
Each hope, each dream, each scheme I have,
Each possibility,
Can be accomplished when I put
My faith and trust in Thee!

The desire accomplished is sweet to the soul. . . .

Proverbs 13:19

... whatsoever things are true,
whatsoever things are honest ...
if there be any virtue, and
if there be any praise, think on these things.

Philippians 4:8

Weeding God's Garden

A seed of dishonesty
can sprout and grow like a weed
choking flowers in a beautiful garden.

Keep me, God,
from sowing such a seed . . .
Help me keep the weeds
out of Your beautiful garden of life!

Serve Him Happily

Grant me, God,
    Wisdom so that
    I may know
    In what ways
    I need to grow!

Grant me, God,
    Vision so that
    I may see
    How to serve
    You happily!

Serve the Lord with gladness. . . .

Psalms 100:2

Another Look

A critic's job is easy,
It's not hard to criticize—
But when you're on the "taking" end,
That's where the trouble lies
For it's often hard to see ourselves
In someone else's eyes . . .
So, when you are corrected,
Don't take it as a blow,
But take correction graciously,
For in your heart you know
The better person you become,
The closer to God you grow!

**Behold, happy is the man whom
God correcteth: therefore
despise not thou the chastening
of the Almighty.**

Job 5:17

Enfolded in God's Love

The good Lord watches
over me
His power protects me
His light surrounds me
His love enfolds me

        Whatever I do
        He is with me

        Wherever I am,
        God is

The Lord is my keeper
and through Him, I live!

For God hath not given us the spirit of fear; but of power, and of love, and of a sound mind.

2 Timothy 1:7

Be Optimistic

You can take your dearest dreams and expectations
And turn each one of them into reality
If you have faith and hold no reservations
And use optimism as a magic key . . .
Erase the words "I can't" and "I'm defeated"
Replace them with "I can" and then you'll see
With faith in God your tasks and goals completed
For with God there's no impossibility!

. . . for with God all things are possible.

Mark 10:27

Obey His Commandments

Children don't know right from wrong,
They need parental care
To teach them and to guide them
With a set of rules to share—
Rules to keep them out of harm,
Rules to help them grow,
Rules that bring a happy heart
To those they love and know—
We are all God's children
And what gladness comes our way
When we follow His commandments
And obey His laws each day!

**Blessed are they that do his
commandments, that they may
have right to the tree of life,
and may enter in through the
gates into the city.**

Revelation 22:14

Wings of Faith

In the sky
an eagle soars
and rides the winds up high

I, too, can fly
and ride the winds of life
because I have wings of faith

Faith in God
who made the eagle,
made the sky
and made the winds of life
to fly!

**For the Lord shall be thy
confidence. . . .**

Proverbs 3:26

Let Me Serve You, Lord

This is my prayer to You, Oh Lord,
This is my fervent prayer . . .
Let me toil in Your vineyard,
Let me more than do my share . . .

Let me walk the straight and narrow,
Let me follow in Your way,
Let me rise to meet the challenges
You've planned for me each day . . .

Let my heart and mind be open,
Let my eyes be open wide,
Let me understand Your wonders,
Let me feel You deep inside . . .

And, when my mortal days are done
And You have sent for me,
Let me serve You with my spirit
For all eternity.

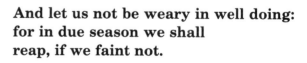

**And let us not be weary in well doing:
for in due season we shall
reap, if we faint not.**

Galatians 6:9

Truth

The truth
is often searched for
in the most obscure places
when it's right before
our eyes.

Teach us
to really see, God,
not only with open eyes
but with open minds
as well.

Behold, thou desirest truth in the inward parts: and in the hidden part thou shalt make me to know wisdom.

Psalms 51:6

Snow Ballet

Listen to the sounds
   listen to the sounds of wintertime
      the whistling,
         howling,
         humming
      of playing winds . . .
a symphony of sounds
   to which a million
         jillion
               dancing snowflakes
         pirouette and bow.

Wintertime . . .
   composed
      conducted
         and choreographed
            by God!

Awake, O north wind. . . .
Song of Solomon 4:16

Have Good Intentions

We all have good intentions
As we begin a day,
We're thankful for God's teachings
And we want to walk His way . . .
But in our daily struggles,
We sometimes fail to show
The virtues He has taught us
To those we love and know . . .
So, as you start a busy day,
Be sure to schedule, too,
Some time for caring, sharing,
And a thoughtful deed to do . . .
And all the love that you bestow,
The kindness that you give,
Will return a hundredfold
To bless the days you live.

. . . man looketh on the outward
appearance, but the Lord
looketh on the heart.

1 Samuel 16:7

Sowing Love

Flowers blooming row by row
Delight the soul and eye—
And other gardens can be sown
That also beautify . . .
Plant a row of kindness,
A row of helpful deeds,
Plant a row to give away
To fill somebody's needs,
Plant a row of thoughtfulness,
A row or two of love—
And you will have a garden
That will rival those above!

And the Lord God took the man, and put him into the garden of Eden to dress it and to keep it.

Genesis 2:15

Trust in Him

As a sailor
trusts a beacon
in unfamiliar waters,
trust in the Lord.

He will bring you through fathomless seas
filled with billowing waves,
through rocky beds and narrow inlets
until you anchor once more
safely in His port.

**. . . for he hath said, I will never leave
thee, nor forsake thee.**

Hebrews 13:5

Be Generous

The more you share and give away,
The more you will be blessed,
A seed of kindness will return
Bouquets of happiness . . .
Try as you may, you can't outgive,
You can't outlove our Lord,
For every generous thing you do
Brings back a rich reward!

**Cast thy bread upon the waters:
for thou shalt find it after
many days.**

Ecclesiastes 11:1

Welcome, Stranger

Open the door
to your home
and welcome
a stranger . . .

Open the door
to your heart
and welcome
a friend!

**Be not forgetful to entertain
strangers: for thereby some
have entertained angels unawares.**

Hebrews 13:2

Be Just

Before you pass a judgment
On a fellow human being,
Make sure you have the broadest view
Of everything you're seeing . . .
Use kindness and forbearance,
Use understanding, too—
The qualities that God would use
If He were judging you!

That which is altogether just shalt
thou follow. . . .

Deuteronomy 16:20

Proud Expressions

If you're proud of your beliefs,
Write them down for all to see—
Not with pen and paper,
But write them eloquently,
With thoughtful deeds, compassion,
With love, with mercy, too,
And your pride in your beliefs
Will shine—along with you!

Thou hast made known to me the
ways of life; thou shalt make
me full of joy with thy countenance.

Acts 2:28

Teaching, Reaching

Teach me, God,
   so I may teach
     Your holy master plan!

Help me, God,
   so I may reach
     everyone I can!

Show me, God,
   how I may find
     the words that most inspire—
Words of goodness
   words of grace
     that lift the spirit higher!

**For God giveth to a man that
is good in his sight wisdom,
and knowledge, and joy....**

Ecclesiastes 2:26

Winter Feast

Some crumbs
for the winter birds
thrown lightly upon the snow
became a large meal
for them.

Spring came
and every morning
with the rising of the sun
they sing a sweet song
of thanks!

**Be thou diligent to know
the state of thy flocks. . . .**

Proverbs 27:23

Be Tolerant

Tolerance is . . .
    The ability
      to see things
        from another's point of view,
    It's knowing
      that we each have
        different values to pursue—
    It's opening your heart
      as God has opened His to you . . .
        that's tolerance!

**Let us therefore follow after the
things which make for peace,
and things wherewith one may edify
another.**

Romans 14:19

Golden Rays of Hope

When your heart is sorely aching,
When you've too much to endure,
When you're weary of your burdens
And you're looking for a cure . . .
Put your faith in God who loves you
And with golden rays of hope,
He will comfort you and give you strength
To climb the steepest slope!

I will not leave you comfortless;
I will come to you.

John 14:18

104

Set a Good Example

"Do as I say, *not* as I do"—
What a foolish point of view!
To make a point to those you teach,
You must practice what you preach . . .
Set good examples day by day,
And then sincerely you can say—
"Do as I say *and* as I do"
To everyone who follows you!

**A good name is rather to be chosen
than great riches, and loving favour
rather than silver and gold.**

Proverbs 22:1

Blessed is the man that trusteth
in the Lord, and whose hope
the Lord is.

Jeremiah 17:7

Have Hope

It's hope
that paints
a rainbow
when a cloudburst fills your sky . . .
It's hope
that brings
some comfort
when teardrops fill your eyes . . .

God gives us hope so we might chase
     away our fears and sorrows—
God gives us hope so we might face
     each challenge of tomorrow!

A New Leaf

Tomorrow
I'll turn over
a new leaf.

I've said that
so many times, Lord,
that by now I've accumulated
enough leaves
to clothe a tree!

Tomorrow isn't soon enough.
Help me get started today, Lord,
help me get started now!

**By much slothfulness the building
decayeth; and through idleness
of the hands the house droppeth
through.**

Ecclesiastes 10:18

Visit the Sick

When someone's sick or sick at heart
And has steep hills to climb,
The nicest get-well present
Is the gift of giving time . . .
Time to write a little note
That says you understand,
Time to sit and chat a bit,
Time to hold a hand,
Time to bring a smile, a word,
Perhaps a hand-picked flower—
Little blessings, gifts of time,
And all have healing power!

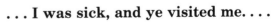

. . . I was sick, and ye visited me. . . .

Matthew 25:36

Keep the Sabbath

Sabbath—
a day to rest
from the hurry-scurry rush
of everyday life.

Sabbath—
a day to reflect,
to stop and think about
where you're going
and where you've been.

Sabbath—
a day to celebrate
God's glorious work of creation,
to commemorate
His day of rest.

Sabbath—
a day to rejoice,
to sing His praises—
to feel God's love!

**Six days thou shalt do thy work,
and on the seventh day thou
shalt rest. . . .**

Exodus 23:12

A Cherished Gift

A compliment is like a gift—
A gift that's heaven-sent,
Especially one that's from the heart
And most sincerely meant . . .
It can't be boxed, it can't be wrapped,
Nor bought in any store,
But it's one gift that everyone
Is always thankful for!

A man hath joy by the answer of
his mouth: and a word spoken
in due season, how good is it.

Proverbs 15:23

Time to Pray

There's time for caring, sharing, dreaming,
Time for working, planning, scheming,
There's time for loving, time for growing,
Time for learning, time for knowing . . .
From joy, to overcoming strife,
There's time for everything in life,
And when we pause awhile to pray,
We spend our time the sweetest way!

**To every thing there is a season, and a
time to every purpose under the heaven.**

Ecclesiastes 3:1

Love Your Parents

Parenthood is patience,
Guidance and advice,
Comfort and devotion,
Concern and sacrifice . . .
Parenthood is thoughtfulness,
It's always being near
To understand, to listen,
To hug away a tear . . .
Parenthood is everything
That's wonderful and fine,
But most of all it's love—because
It's part of God's design!

**Thy father and thy mother shall
be glad, and she that bare
thee shall rejoice.**

Proverbs 23:25

Keep thy heart with all diligence; for out of it are the issues of life.

Proverbs 4:23

Dew Drop

In an early morning hour,
A drop of dew formed on a flower,
It glistened in the sun, and then
Joining others on the stem
It fell with them onto the ground
And headed toward a stream it found.

Over rocky beds it went
To where a river gently bent.
Then onward to the ocean blue
Flowed the little drop of dew.

And when a mist formed it was there
And rose into the evening air.

Then in an early morning hour
The drop of dew formed on a flower
And glistened in the sun . . .

A lesson, God, in diligence
And faith for everyone!

Serenity

God created still blue lakes,
Slowly drifting clouds,
Shady glens, and mountaintops
Far away from crowds . . .
So, when you're feeling pressured
And you want to feel serene,
Just close your eyes and visualize
Your favorite quiet scene . . .
And when you're feeling calm once more
You'll feel God's presence near
And in that peaceful state of mind
Your cares will disappear!

. . . be not dismayed; for I am thy God:
I will strengthen thee. . . .

Isaiah 41:10

A Heavy Load

The burdens of guilt
  of sin and remorse
    are heavy loads to bear . . .
The Lord knows this,
  He understands,
    He loves you and He cares . . .
So go before Him
  and confess
    your errors, omissions and slips,
And He'll forgive you
  as the words
    are being formed on your lips . . .
Then He'll guide you
  and He'll help you
    correct your wrongdoings, and then
Your burden will be lighter
  as you walk
    in His pathway again!

**If we confess our sins, he is faithful
and just to forgive us our sins and
to cleanse us from all unrighteousness.**

1 John 1:9

Be Humble

When I blossom, God,
it is only because
I have my roots
planted firmly in You.

Your golden rays of hope
have been sunshine to me,
Your words of wisdom
have nurtured me,
Your trials and tests
have strengthened me.

Without You, God,
I would fade and wither
and dry.

With You, God,
I live,
I grow,
I blossom!

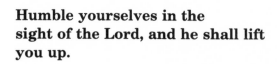

**Humble yourselves in the
sight of the Lord, and he shall lift
you up.**

James 4:10

Keep a Pure Heart

Let no sounds escape my lips, Lord,
Except words of good will,
Lead me in the way of righteousness,
Let evil thoughts be stilled,
Help me do my best for others,
Help me, Lord, to make a start
To do Your bidding always
And to purify my heart!

Blessed are the pure in heart: for they shall see God.

Matthew 5:8

119

Forgive Others

God gave a tough assignment
For all of us to do—
To pray for all those who hurt us,
And to love our enemies, too . . .
So, when other people wrong you,
Instead of striking back,
Say a little prayer for them.
For qualities they lack . . .
Ask the Lord to give them
An extra portion of
Insight and compassion—
And to bless them with His love.

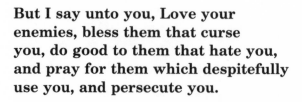

But I say unto you, Love your
enemies, bless them that curse
you, do good to them that hate you,
and pray for them which despitefully
use you, and persecute you.

Matthew 5:44

Reflections

Dear God,
I've noticed
a peculiar thing
about mirrors.
How I see myself
depends upon the light
in which I view myself—
the brighter the light,
the truer the image.

Dear God,
to see my inner self,
let me view myself in Your light
so the image will be true,
and I can see what I need to do
to be a better person—
to be a reflection
of You!

. . . old things are passed away;
behold, all things are become new.

2 Corinthians 5:17

Rejoice at a Rainbow

The earth is newly washed from rain
Still clinging in the air,
Bringing a fragrance of freshness
As it touches everywhere,
And as the rain prepares to leave,
Before the clouds depart,
We're treated to a showing
From God's gallery of art—
Multicolor hues form
An archway in the sky,
Uplifting hearts and spirits,
Delighting every eye . . .
For all who see God's rainbow
Know it's a token of
A Covenant between our Lord
And those who share His love!

**I do set my bow in the cloud, and
it shall be for a token of a
covenant between me and the earth.**

Genesis 9:13

Marvel at His Miracles

We don't
have to see
a burning bush
or a parting sea
to witness God's miracles.

A budding bush,
a fish-filled sea
are miracles.

Night and day,
and changing seasons,
technology,
and minds that reason—
all of these are miracles.

Inch by inch,
and minute by minute
life has nothing
but miracles in it!

**Remember his marvellous
works that he hath done. . . .**

Psalms 105:5

Love Yourself

If you can say, "I love You, God!"
With your heart, your soul, and might,
If you believe God's power,
His mercy, goodness and light,
Then it's natural to love yourself
And believe in all you do—
For you are truly part of God,
And God is part of you!

Hereby know we that we dwell
in him, and he in us, because
he hath given us of his Spirit.

1 John 4:13

I Love You, God!

For creating
every atom,
every star,
and every flower,
            and for putting
            me among them
            with my own
            creative power . . .
                    I love You, God!

As my
faithful friend,
my Father,
and my ever-guiding light,
            with all my being,
            all my soul,
            with all my heart
            and might . . .
                    I love You, God!

**And thou shalt love the Lord thy
God with all thine heart,
and with all thy soul, and with
all thy might.**

                    Deuteronomy 6:5